for my family & for Anna

FIELDGLASS

Crab Orchard Series in Poetry
First Book Award

FIELDGLASS

Catherine Pond

Crab Orchard Review & Southern Illinois University Press
Carbondale

Southern Illinois University Press
www.siupress.com

24 23 22 21   4 3 2 1

Front and back cover art: Brian Merriam

The Crab Orchard Series in Poetry is a joint publishing venture of Southern
Illinois University Press and *Crab Orchard Review*. This series has been made
possible by the generous support of the Office of the President of Southern
Illinois University and the Office of the Vice Chancellor for Academic Affairs
and Provost at Southern Illinois University Carbondale.

Editor of the Crab Orchard Series in Poetry, 1998–2019: Jon Tribble
Judge for the 2020 First Book Award: Traci Brimhall
For queries and submissions, contact Allison Joseph: aljoseph@siu.edu

Library of Congress Cataloging-in-Publication Data
Names: Pond, Catherine, 1989– author.
Title: Fieldglass / Catherine Pond.
Description: Carbondale : Crab Orchard Review ; Southern Illinois
    University Press, [2021] | Series: Crab Orchard series in poetry
Identifiers: LCCN 2020027979 (print) | LCCN 2020027980 (ebook) |
    ISBN 9780809338146 (paperback ; recycled paper) |
    ISBN 9780809338153 (ebook)
Subjects: LCGFT: Poetry.
Classification: LCC PS3616.O588 F54 2021 (print) |
    LCC PS3616.O588 (ebook) | DDC 811/.6—dc23
LC record available at https://lccn.loc.gov/2020027979
LC ebook record available at https://lccn.loc.gov/2020027980

We look at the world once, in childhood.
The rest is memory.

—Louise Glück

… how cold it was
and how often I walked to the edge of the actual
river to join you

—Franz Wright

CONTENTS

FIELDGLASS

LIKE RAIN

My father digs me out of snow with a shovel.
With the record player on, or alone in my room

I trace the invisible illness growing inside me.
You come and then you go like summer rain.

You come and then you go. I float hands-free
over an altar of knives. You come and then

you go like summer rain. You come and then
you go. Like rain. Like rain. Like summer rain.

I'M A YOUNG COWBOY AND KNOW I'VE DONE WRONG

I'm a young cowboy and know I've done wrong,
my father sang as I emerged from the river.

She likes wearing men's clothes, let her wear them,
said my mother, tying his denim shirt around my neck.

Under the surface of the water, rocks glimmered
like small hearts. Here's the mountain

where we stood in order of height, stars flashing
across our faces. What my father could not give my mother

she gave to herself. I wanted to be like that;
like the lawnmower, commanding respect, a steady echo.

Instead I was more like the grass, in love
with being severed, and later, with finding those parts

of myself that had been buried, thin blades
only the fresh spring rain had the power to recover.

MONHEGAN

Ledged in a memory
of being moored, what chafes
at the edge of the wharf

answers no. Spring tide,
neap tide, against-tide, still the kiss
is what you current for most.

Rumrunner
coursing the mouth, scraping bottom,
teething at the keel. Come closer,

winter is over. This sudden foam,
this rush, this third-quarter moon,
these are for you

and they come only once.
How fast. And with how many hulls.

My father is dreamy, forgetful, aloof. But I've never actually been left
behind before. I walk behind an aisle of Frito Lays and burst into tears.

I should've eaten the eggs he bought me at the Super 8. I should've saved
my allowance like he'd said. I should've made myself bigger, louder,

less forgettable. A female customer has her eyes locked on me as she speaks
into her boxy cellphone: *Yes, maybe two minutes ago. Looks about ten,*

barefoot, wearing pink pajamas. It takes about five minutes, but Dad
still beats the cops back to the station. His arms are too tan from years

on the water, moles dark as moons, and he takes me in them gingerly,
as if I am already dead, and because I've never heard him cry I whisper,

It's okay, daddy, I'm okay. He smells of unwashed denim and paint thinner.
He doesn't notice the people staring, or the cop car rolling slow motion

into the station, or the woman watching our reunion with her hands
over her mouth, relief that I am not actually abandoned,

although at some point, I will be, we will all be, as she knows,
as she too has been abandoned. I am eleven and lucky. No one is yet dead.

It will be months before anyone dies. *God forgive me,* he whispers
into my child's ear, and I realize in this scenario, I am the God

to whom he speaks. I could wield my power, but won't. Mom is across
the country. Dad wears a gold chain around his neck. I reach for it.

ALEXEI

More than once I found him bleeding uncontrollably.
Bleeding in his bed, bleeding against the walls.

In pain, we were inadequate, though I was quieter,
healthier I suppose. Once, I found him shuffling in my tutu,

fondling his crotch under the milky tulle.
He knew before I did what the world held in store.

My brother, little Tsarevitch in women's clothes.
Afternoons, the doctor spoke to him; I was permitted

only to watch, rake the sand back and forth
in its stupid box. I felt sorry for my father.

When you write to your mother, he said,
remember to tell her how happy we are.

The next week we sat together
on the ledge, listening.

Institutionalize said my father's voice. *No*
said my mother's voice.

Enabling him said my father's voice. *Fuck
you* said my mother's voice.

Then the screaming, muffled, like someone had put a sheet
over someone else's mouth.

Then the sound of something shattering.

When I began to cry, my brother turned from me slowly
like a piece of machinery

and closed the door to his room.

That night, he played Rachmaninoff
on the piano until dawn.

From above I watched his dark hair, dangling
over the keys, and Dad's painting

behind him—a nautical scene—all that water,
rising and falling along the living room wall,

F A N T A S Y in bright red letters
across the side of the boat.

A birch tree foams out over the breakwater.
Peace was a rain thick as milk, mute colors of an endless causeway.

Shut up, my brother used to say to the air. *Shut up, shut up.*
But I could never hear the song inside his head.

Happiness was there, though out of reach, like a river,
tracing the land alongside us.

*

IN THE SULFUR BATHS

Under coronets of steam, the other women watch you lower in.
Wasps bloom at the edges. You've lost weight, you are aware.

Your collarbone holds its own shape. The other women are excitable,
whispering about men. They want to know what you used to tell yourself

late at night about a princedom in the hills—who you loved—
who braided your puritan hair   —you have nothing for them.

You cover your breasts with both hands. Across the pool,
a woman strokes the sweat from her face. There is an ironwork gate

behind her, a row of blue elms when she pulls back her hair.
You alone see the horse appear, baring its teeth in the mist.

TATIANA

White taffeta circled her waist
looped with a thin brown belt. I reached out and slid
my hand under. Don't,
she said. We're sisters.

Outside the castle, the kingdom
fluttered apart. Blues and reds and golds
bled out against the snow. Our mother

had lost her mind. She had found
religion. At night I watched through the keyhole
as she lowered herself
in front of the bearded starets. I didn't know about
sex. I was in love

with my sister.
This was before Tsarskoye Selo,
before Yekaterinburg,
before I watched her body drop
into my lap like a piece
of driftwood, all that dark hair
against my hand.

I wish I was a lesbian, she said. I tried, you know.
I nodded, I know. She turned toward the window

and closed her eyes. Her hair, still damp from rain,
was darker than usual. Behind her, a field

was revealing itself: grey heather along the road,
an abandoned house, green wheat

where the water began. I'm sorry, she said.
I just miss him. Later, she woke from a nap

to the sound of rain and touched her head gently
to my shoulder. Don't get sick of me, she said.

Deer in bright snow.
Darkness like a centrifuge

spins, pulls everything toward the edges.
The trick is not to care

when she kisses me. Not to touch
the death drive passing back and forth

between us. Any day now.
Heat rises under my eyes.

In the restaurant neon signs face outward
advertising beer. *Genesee, Schaefer.*

In another life she leaves him.
We kiss until the windows gleam with rain

or night empties into the soft whoosh
of cars along the state road.

Snow flanks the street, shoveled in piles higher than my head. It was the winter
of lost gloves and ear infections, of iced-over porch parties, of long johns.

I lived with four girls. In the photo, my nails are Pepto pink, and the girls gather
around me, faces blurry in the frame. I remember the smell of their perfume—

Jo Malone, Chloe, Marc Jacobs—and the lime-basil scent of liquid soap
I stole handfuls of in our shared shower. That was happiness. We kissed

the lips of cold bottles, or we kissed each other. We slept curled against
one another in the dark. Late at night, death introduced itself, casually at first,

like a slant of light under the bedroom door. Cecile stood in the snow,
heaving drifts off the windshield of her car. Cornelia taped a woodcut print

to my window. When they hauled her off to rehab, I drew a house on a hill,
thin and haunted. Scarlet was the first to get sober. I don't blame her

for not coming back. I tried living anywhere after that. Still, when I close
my eyes, I see snow. Piles of silvery clothes. I hear the clink of the beaded

curtains, the low whisper of voices at night, calling from room to room.

That town was the same when I finally returned:
hay bales belted down by frost, hillsides glassy.

River heavy with porcelain plates. The pine trees
stood tall in their refusal, antique, undiagnosed.

I was afraid to forgive you, alone, narcotic
in that collapsing house. Bandstand glowing

like a dollhouse in a dream. You were a child
with me. Each year I came home from the city

and the landscape seemed less lucid.
The ice broke and reformed.

The moon stood watch over my motel,
like a sister appearing silently in the doorway.

You like sex with other women
because it makes you feel safe,
she says. Nothing makes me
feel safe, I explain. She is married

but when her daughter wins
the fishing contest at Sacandaga,
she offers me the prize trout.
Later, loosening the flesh

from the spine, I do not feel
relieved, or thankful. She who knows
me best believed I might be
nourished by this small, dead thing.

Snow fell forever
in that room
and the heater moaned
in the electrical closet.
For both of us,
there existed a boundary
between the mind
and the body.
That was the sort of love
we liked.

You gave me poems
that spoke
to the ways in which
love fails us,
though you were happy
with your husband.

At night I lay in bed
a few blocks
away, listening
to the crinkle
of ice cracking
at the windows.

You had a silver streak
in your hair

like my mother's.
The rest of your hair was black.

Maybe it was my mother
I longed to recover.

Maybe I was the daughter
you'd lost.

One winter
I drove to the lake
alone and walked out
on the ice.
The highway home
was covered in a thin layer
of frozen water,
and my car slid out
into a snow bank. I survived
and didn't mind. I hated existing
in time. One day
I would have to live in the world

without you.
I remember the white kitchen,
the blue tile floor.
Your tea cupboard
had every flavor.
I could never make up my mind
so you chose for me.
In the morning
the tea leaves

were still there
curled in water, and steam rose

off the snow
in shapes

we had no name for.

*

SUMMER HOUSE

For years I let no one touch me. I had myself to preserve.
Not to mention the poems, which, like rocks, refused penetration.

It was a surprise to discover my body, collapsed like a bridge,
but still beautiful, still wet with snow.

Leaves swirled out across the water, glittering
like some ghostly path. I ached, knowing it would end,

first the moonlight, then the clearing it had made,
that empty space between headboard and base where, laughing,

I locked myself between your legs.

Some storms are quiet, an engine starting up.
Others smell of gasoline, rising through the rain,

or have the shape of a truck bed, or shudder like
the wheel against my wrists. You would be unhappy

with me. At night tinder snaps in the stove
against the sound of your voice. We veer toward

a colder season, as at the straightaway, a tarn
vanishes behind a row of jack pines.

Though the reality of other women excited you, fantasies
about them made you feel excluded.
So I came up with scenarios
involving other men. Me, bruised from knots.
Me, over a railing.
One night, as we were walking to dinner,
I had the fantasy I knew I couldn't say.
The avenue was dark, a man lay dead or alive
near the marble fountain.
A foghorn went off in the harbor
and seemed to go on forever, pulsing,
moving closer through the dense, grey night.
The poor ships, I thought, but
nothing could shake the water from my brain.
Cars swam along under the street lamps.
I glided beside you as though roped, my body
displacing the light.
In your eyes I believed I could see
the birches and mild lakes of my childhood.
The challenge of wet surfaces. Cold sedge.
And for the first time I loved this city, though I knew
you would leave me
alone in it. Knew exactly when, and for whom.

Through the glass panel
across the hall,

I see the plane that will take me
out of this life.

I am suddenly very tired. I feel as if
I will cry. The little glass bottle is heavy.
I douse my wrist, my neck,
my hair. I hope he remembers the smell
of my perfume.
I wore it so he would remember me.

I have this nightmare. I'm on a hill,
near a grove of orange trees.
I'm so excited to get inside the grove,
a clean void
where I can sit and write.

But when I part the leaves,
he is already there, answering me
in my own voice.

This painting doesn't get any less ugly
the longer I look at it,
but it's mine. My sadness, my voice
cracked in half,
bright wound around which darkness
arranges itself, like flowers
along the highway—color
at the end of long sadness—
Have you ever walked through years of rooms
of dark canvases
wanting to die?
If so, you know how I feel.
I want to be back in the city,
years from now,
all the dead hearts washed clean by rain.
If I hadn't spent those six seasons
covered in snow
I wouldn't recognize the terrible
burst of hope
in a slash of pink paint—
Georgia in summer, the smell of hydrangea
rotting in the sun. Sweet
and punishing.
If I love you the way I love myself,
I will be ruthless.
Rothko said it was his brightest paintings
that indicated deepest grief.
I never was good at letting go.
By now you know
it is raining. By now you know
I have entered
the room.

The boy that took pictures of me being raped
died a year ago

when he drove his truck into a pond.
He managed to get out of the car but the area was boggy;
he drowned in four feet of water.

So often one has to tone down the truth
in order to be believed.

The truth is, I was always scared of men.
What destroyed me that night
had been destroying me all along.

Now perhaps you understand
why I never told you about this. I liked what you saw
when you looked at me.

I liked telling you stories about the women I'd been with,
I liked turning you on.
I told you all kinds of things. When you left,

I didn't eat for a month.
I couldn't brush my teeth
without throwing up.

Here's the dream I never told—
I wake alone in the grass. I laugh

because I am terrified. It is you
who finds me, puts the towel around me tenderly,
carries me inside.

The sun dips down behind Shaker Mountain, the grey bodies of trees
gleam out from behind the leaves.

*

Forest sleeps with three Samurai swords under his bed, of varying size.
We are friends, nothing more. I am to understand this.

*

He takes me to the opera (*Madama Butterfly*) and touches me in our private
    balcony.

*

The air is dry and cool. Under the streetlights, the highway turns blue. One
    billboard announces
an upcoming comedy show. Another, a suicide hotline.

Beyond them, invisible from the highway, the desert itself: pale and purple at
    this hour.

*

A year passes.

*

Forest wants to introduce me to his girlfriend, but I can't breathe properly when
    I hear her name.

*

The town of Speculator is more of an intersection, comprising a gas station
        (Mountain Market),
a motel (The Cedarhurst Motor Lodge), and a diner (King of the Frosties),
        clustered at the junction
of NYS Route 8 and NYS Route 30.

*

Every weekend, I drive six hours to eat a sandwich alone at this intersection.

*

I sleep with someone new, a filmmaker. *Good for you*, my father says, and means
        it.

*

My father never could make my brother happy. Seventy-four years old, my dad
        stands alone in a circle
of hair, swinging a dusty saw.

*

Snow seals the city. The filmmaker stops calling. *Too bad*, I think, bruising my
        calves at the bar.

*

The sun comes out; I feel the sidewalks and the city-people loosen. They flood
        me gently.

*

Back in Brooklyn, I hold my best friend's baby close to my chest. I see Forest
        from across the room.

*

I walk with him through rows and rows of books. I think about the knives under
    his bed.
I still remember the first time I put his beard in my mouth
and I

*

don't love him any less.

*

I keep an eye out for the delicate paper faces
of the dead. Antlers wrung like scrap paper,
twisting skyward in the mist.
To create you have to be able to kill.
At least that's what my daddy said.
It takes courage to cut your glass-green poison
down to size. If I could see the stars
they might look like you—distant and beautiful,
built up.

There's one thing that keeps us all weak,
and that's hiding in the dark, as if what we have to hide
could be any more shameful
than what we have to show. Alone in the cabin
I hear the bear below, rattling
at the trash. He is all that I have loved
and lost. A child, he plays all night
with the tops of the cans.

REHAB

The guy at my college reunion is incredulous.
I knew you weren't a lesbian, he says.
I laugh like I knew it too. Who cares. Not me.

In Los Angeles I stood on top of the San Andreas fault
and wished so hard for an earthquake, I believed
I could conjure it. Now when I hear the wind you are with me,

the stranger on the stairs, reminding me how little I matter.
It's why I love the stars so much.
I thought if I was good the universe would be good back

but when I'm brushing my teeth the world is one big grey collapse.
There are three of me: the one you love, the one
in the mirror, and the one inside, the worthless one,

who can't rinse her teeth without gagging,
who sits on the toilet wiping mint
and vomit from her mouth. Dad says, I love you.

Get a grip. He offers to pay for another trip to California,
rental car and all, if it will make me happy.
It's cheaper than rehab, he jokes.

But I found a place in Santa Fe
in case it comes to that.

I park outside a local diner, alone in the fog. I brush my hair
but don't feel better. *To be vulnerable is to be in pain.*

I open the car door and see myself staring back
behind the barricade: dimly lit meadow, endless stretch

of mist with a lake in the center. Horses ring the lake.
They sleep standing up. Some days I feel like a plastic carton

drifting between lanes, lifted into a wheel bed,
then crushed. I haven't had sex in months. I remember

the first: I wanted to practice on someone I didn't love,
so it wouldn't matter if there was any blood.

Now this landscape, this old layering
technique. A mountain range of cut paper,

rustling in my swift, sharp hands. An ounce is
a measurement or a snow leopard, depending.

Slinking in the redder weather, soft pelt withheld.
Why lie, I adored you. See the way I hold my wrists.

Rain falls in milligrams, where I tell you secrets
I can't tell myself. I get sick of just about everyone.

My body wants for the first love, administered
only in increments I am capable of, or I can conjure.

Rain rumples the maples. One leaf dangles
and drops, loose button, from a string of rain.

It is not a serious loss, though the lake swells,
blue and ready, filling the leafy eyelets.

Tired of the upright world, a loon slides
gracefully under. I am not so easily won.

The old fears squat quietly, hands folded,
inside my stomach. Oh, what could you do

to me now. The hound with the humped
torso, see how he sleeps at my side.

Some nights I run naked from bed
and put on the trees like green raincoats.

It's the oldest dream. I'm not asking permission.

*

I was so dumb. I thought your suffering was something
I could solve, or at least

push out of sight,
like the dead falcon we found in the forest and carried back

home under steel-blue
night to bury.

I thought death was a story we'd tell ourselves later,
and laugh. Instead, you stopped

sharing things with me,
except the poems, which I didn't even know you'd been

writing. I was your only
reader. That summer in the High Peaks your drafts piled up

on the picnic table
under a paperweight,

edges shimmering in the wind like long, silver wings.
You were newly thirteen.

I was halfway
through eleven. I began to write back.

I thought we could live together this way,
side by side,

not speaking, watching ink run like waves across the page.
How could we have known

what the water would do, that the depth pressure
would pull us apart, that time

would come toward us, soundless, amorphous.
That love is an agony

we enter alone.

GRIEF

The ugliness was beginning. Those days
I was already drinking, and you did not

like to be touched. The thing is, I was happy.

Sometimes light washed the side of your face
in a glow. There was a cathedral, I remember,

and a river where you rowed, where the trees

bent to touch the water and a mist spread thin
across the surface. In the mornings

I'd go down to the shore and watch you glide

out in the chill, past the split oak, toward
the grey, tremulous center.

The day your brother dies I undress,
bury the clothes I'm wearing

in the trash. A long-sleeve striped shirt
and a pair of jeans. It's

October. I don't know how you feel,
what you throw out.

The lake falls back into itself
like a first draft.

*

You start sleeping on the floor.
When I spend the night

I join you, the two of us
cocooned in comforters. All night I listen

for your breath from beneath
the blue-grey chrysalis.

*

At home, my mom starts reading to me
in the evening again. She has

a clear voice, like water.
I'm getting too old for it,

but each night she saves
a space for me

in bed beside her.

*

Time behaves strangely, moving forward
and away.

Magnolias bloom like inkblots in the yard.
Drought turns the willow

yellow in the wind.

*

Somewhere what you love is still alive
turning cartwheels in a gentle snow

is the kind of lie I write years later, wishing
I could make it true for you.

*

Winter sister. Seventeen years
of sleeping on floors.

We live so far apart but I still wake
searching for your shape in the dark.

You still call me in your quiet voice,
waiting and waiting

for what won't come home.

We don't speak. I climb into his truck as if guided
by an invisible hand, as if we've known
each other our whole lives. And we have. The rain
picks up as we drive, and the street signs

change color, then shape. When we reach the turnoff,
the road is light grey, almost transparent,
like a worn-out piece of paper. He leads me up
the concrete steps and into the house.

I take it all in: The paint-wrecked furniture. The slurry
for casting, sand melted down in a fluidized bed,
shelves lined with bronze objects. Backyard overrun
with scrap metal and half-finished sculptures.

An electricity moves between us, as if time were a map
that's been leading me back to this town
made peaceful by rain, and all those years without him
seem like a joke, bruised and piled

together like plums in a bowl. Outside, he throws open
the garage to show me his father's Corvette,
which he's kept in good condition. It sparkles
like a dark forest, the rearview mirrors

like miniature lakes. I remember our long rides
through wealthy neighborhoods, how his dad
let me and Anna hang off the back of the convertible
and slide around turns, the mansions

boring compared to the bounce and burn of the speeding car.
Hop in, he says, and I do.
I feel safe with him, whooshing along the back roads,
the secret of our childhood a rope between us,

so when we stop at the cemetery and get out to walk,
I stay close at his side. What is it like,
I ask him finally, when we reach the headstone
with his name on it. Lilies have grown up

around the grave, and he picks one and puts it in my hair.
It's quiet, he says. His hand
is huge on top of mine. His loneliness moves
through my body like a pulse, and I can't remember

whether it was prescription pills or heroin, suicide
or an accident. It doesn't matter anymore.
In this version, he's alive. We have our whole lives
ahead of us.

1

and when I loved you with all my will   my will

wasn't enough   and when I closed my eyes
I saw railroad tracks glittering in the rain

the road to Dahlonega dotted with gold we panned for
in the river   all those towns with names like birds

Aska, Ellijay, Jasper

2

you spoke of him in present tense for a decade
after his death and I did too   I was going to love you

harder than Heaven could   I was going to keep you
close to me on Earth   but you found different ways

to disappear   and maybe I loved you all along
maybe there was no one else   maybe I loved you all along

twin-sister, trestle, hurt when I was young   hurt so bad
I couldn't speak, and Lily, frostbitten by the time

we found her

3

now your voice glows in the dark   now even
the flames are distant, eating up someone else's house

now there's a winter where we can meet
where memory won't hold us by the wrists: a windstorm

we can sleep beneath   but when I loved you
with all my will   my will wasn't enough

and when I closed my eyes I saw railroad tracks
glittering in the rain   the road to Dahlonega
still dotted with gold we panned for in the river

all those towns with names like birds
Aska, Ellijay, Jasper

Under a replica of a mammoth sloth, you place my hand
on your stomach and I feel the baby
kick. I look at a diorama of the Canadian Prairie, imagine

a tornado sweeping across the cardboard empire,
shaking the figurines loose from their toothpick fence.
We don't speak; the museum

of tomorrow is small, and we are scared of the surgical knife
that will slice through your abdomen.
To exit, we walk backward through the Devonian era

where the world is mostly water
and you get tired quickly. Here, the fish are still just
forming. The first forests, taking shape.

*

You have sex like someone that's been raped,
he told me.
For once, it felt good to be strapped
to a moving target. To feel
the rock-heavy bones buoying me up,
each gallop shattering
my pudendum past the grey-green river,
the broken estuary.
When we reached an impasse, I stroked
the silvery mane once
before being thrown into
a pile of hay, the golden filaments collapsing
around my body
like a million arms, or like two, yours,
and there you were,
where you had been waiting,
turning blue in the shadow
from the barn, with all the sculptures you had ever made
while I was asleep.
How beautiful, how forever, I thought,
taking your rough
hands in mine.
And I wanted to hate the horse that almost killed me,
carrying me to you,
but I had to love him, too,
because he carried me.

Just yesterday
the sky was blue and blank.
Now it's filled with sound, with white streaks.
Sound splits the day
into parts, rattling the ground.
Spectators crowd the streets.
I imagine they are the same people who like roller coasters,
who invite the excitement
of an earthquake.
How they gasp happily, watching the trick planes
rise and fall above them
feeling the cold calm of being still on Earth
while the wings switchblade
across the sky, such clean coordinates.
Toward sunset the wings vanish
like ripples in water, and all those years
spent trying to make you laugh
unravel like exhaust,
leaving behind nothing but sky and collapsible
stars, visible to us only
as a flat field. You need a telescope
to tell the difference
in time. Now you sleep in my arms
like a sailboat tucked in its slip
though somewhere I can't see, you are still
lowering yourself down
in a windy dark, watching
the world through a small windshield,
speckled with frost —
snow blowing over Lake Superior
in the space between a long silence
and a burst of sound. I want to love you
in no particular order.
It's okay to love what's still alive

Once, drunk, I said I hated
men's hands, how dirty they are,
how they put all that dirt inside you.
Listening to Skrillex on the drive down
from Saratoga I think on how I love you,
but how I love driving more:
the speed, the blur, how nice it feels
to exist outside of time. How like death.
I've always loved a good dream.
But now I want something real.
It took you the full forty-five minutes
from Kingston, wrists balanced
on the wheel, to work the resin out
from under your nails with a blade.
Later, you made a joke about it,
but I'd never seen your hands so clean.

You show me your drawings of single-shots, Colts,
double-barrels. Then you hold up a real one.
A bullet cracks the air, like a hull in ice.
I try to hide my surprise. Still, I can taste your smile.
Around the time of the shootings I started blacking out
on airplanes, subway trains, even in bed.
I paced the sidewalks half asleep, like a woman
waiting to be blown into a star.
How romantic, I used to think, to die still beautiful,
a buck in velvet. But time changes things.
The last time I visited, you unveiled
your newest sculpture, a pistol cast in bronze.
It glowed like an amulet. Dim slips of streetlight
clung to it like rainwater. Later that night,
you jiggled my body easily, like a sheet,
into a position you liked. Darkness pooled
in the soft shallows of my hips. Don't take it
so personally, you said, the day Paris
was attacked. When you touched me I felt grateful,
like a child who'd been given a gift.
Grateful even, when you braced your arms against
the mattress, looked right through me
to the bare earth below.

There's a string of bells in my brain. They hurt me.
Like a child I sleep
uninvited under the big white quilt on your couch.
I sleep like a swan
twisting in a lash of snow. In the morning
I should go and I should
take my raincoat with me. The castle on the hill
blurs in the mist,
the lamps spill onto the lawn. Outside your house
I smash a puddle
open with my boot and send a small wave into the street.
Admit you despise me,
despise my body. It glows like the river, it rises up
in your dreams, it is everything
you walked away from. And you think
you are the monastery,
the tall mountain from which my nerves
dangle, a string of bells
to be cut clean.

In the dream, as in life, my dog drowns.
It isn't a metaphor. Just pain I have no power over.

Just another November spent in bed
trying to control the weather with my mind.

All summer I've been watching you walk out
onto the ice, waiting for it to break,

looking down at the world frozen under glass:
kelp and fish, shells, shattered bottles.

Long ago the doctor promised me a better life.
When I fell in love, she said, *Don't undo the work we've done*

but I was already dreaming of you beside me
in a dark wood away from the world.

Now I fly back to the old city and stand in her doorway
watching rain fall on the streets below.

Now I want to hold her, tell her I missed her,
tell her how hard it's been. I want to say,

Without you, sorrow has no center. Instead,
I smooth my long black coat into quarters

and like a lover say, *It's been so long.*

*

I wear my loneliness lightly, like a little plastic
poncho. In the evening when the park clears out,
the moon swells, mercurial. I am on medicine
for the visions, and so that I will not obsessively
check the news and the weather, as I have done
for the past 22 years. Sometimes the medicine works
and sometimes it doesn't. The fact remains
that it's warmer than ever: 76 degrees today
in Central Park. A silver maple burns beneath
the bridge. A sailboat comes apart in the pond.
Yesterday, a boy with a name like a poet
was stabbed to death in a spree in Jaffa.
We hear about him because he is American.
I imagine him crumpled on a staircase
above the Mediterranean, facedown
on the soapstone steps, like Maria Hassabi
mid-dance. Picture the sea from the top of the stairs,
pouring out beneath his body. When asked
about Mahmoud Darwish, Yehuda Amichai
said he did not agree with his politics,
but conceded that they shared a sea, a desert,
and a deep hatred of the other's ideals.
We are, he admitted, writing almost the same
poems. Poetry becomes more popular
in times of crisis. By this logic I should be thrilled
to learn that herpes causes Alzheimer's,
lead is seeping into the water supply
in Newark, and Zika continues to spread
in Brazil. Picture the sea from the top
of the stairs, pouring out beneath his body.
The American's last name was *FORCE*,
like how you took me one night, gently, then violently,
the hard push into tomorrow a thin veil
for love. But now that you're here, why not

take my heart. Sandstone, stuffed full
of letters, jammed and trampled and fortified
as the Western Wall. Go on. It's the smallest corner
with the highest stakes. We'll die soon
anyway. I'm giving it to you to take.

October 31st, Lützschena. The sky looks like snowfall but nothing comes.
In our host family there are three daughters: Johanna, Maja, and Greta.

Beyond the castle is a park, and in the park a river. We step over a basket
of apples to get to the bikes. We pedal past Auwald Station under black alder,

bird cherry, ash. We pedal past the pond, the statue of Diana. Horses scooping
the air with soft noses. I grew up in a house near a horse farm.

Rain polished the days into perfect puddles, but when I looked too closely
at my reflection, there was always something about to break.

Now night falls, translucent as water. When I blink, my eyelashes
clarify the darkness, like the rubber wipers in a car wash.

Love isn't lupine, those divided leaves which die in winter. It isn't purple
or ash-pink. It's telescope glass: you can see across to the other side.

Saxony, where the farmers make wooden figurines in winter
when the fields are frozen and the Earth gives nothing back.

Each figurine holds a wooden flower. Know that whenever a force is exerted
from outside, there is also a force being exerted from within,

which amplifies the pressure. I don't know where the original owners
of the castle went during the war. The photos stop at 1938.

In the Jewish Museum, the photo that pains me most is the pile of eyeglasses.
When the Soviets took over, the castle went into disrepair.

Birch trees grew up out of the floor, rain made little mountain streams
down the marble staircase. In the morning: mist, steam, rain.

Rain ribboning over the brown earth. Rain slack-jawed
against the windows. Steam on the inside pane of the shower

where I write my name. Maja is the youngest. At breakfast she sits next to me
and speaks rapid-fire. When I ask her mother to translate,

she shrugs, explains: *She is speaking her own language.*
Later, by the tree house, I draw shapes in water with a thin branch,

and think of the summer we didn't speak. The warm space in bed
where your body was. I bend the stick in my hand.

Nothing ever really breaks, though force can cause a flexible object to deform.

Walking to the cemetery this morning, rain.
And a teakettle and spoon for the bear
if he came back. But I knew
he wouldn't. I drank coffee, made myself
anxious, swam out into the lake.
Still I can't get the glass out of my head you lodged there.
After the end of each semester, Lowell
checked himself into McLean for observation.
Demise of the routine resembling
demise of the self, dried-up feathers,
dumb nest you built your life around.
I miss my students in summer,
their sloppy, elaborate sex scenes,
poems that have nothing to do with the erotic
but with proving to an audience
that someone loves them, someone with a body
to make them complete,
and I give them all an A, because why not,
they're in for worse surprises.
And should there be a confession in the hallway,
should there be tears, I will not tell.
The syntax could use a little work, I will offer,
but the love seemed real.

I study my face in the fluorescent light,
rough and scrubbed bare as a tennis ball.
I've lost track of whether being alone
was a choice. In meetings I sit in a cold
metal chair surrounded by other alcoholics,
my notebook open, scribbling quotes
about self-esteem, but if I bring the wrong pen
the words look like snow piles on an empty page
and I spend the hour angry with myself.
I live in the largest city on the eastern seaboard.
In the fly-over states there's a family
with a 3-car garage and a life I'm embarrassed
to admit I want. They know more than me,
those farmers like fishermen, hauling in
barrels of husks. Salt of the earth, heart of the sea.
You call me only when it is raining
or snowing ash in Calabasas. Better to be
thought of during an apocalypse than not
at all but I can't help picturing you in a field,
somewhere desolate and flat, where the wind
is the only voice you have to reason with.
A lot goes on between here and there.
I've mapped America and there are more cities
than stars. In other words, all kinds of places
we could meet in the middle.

He was gone by then, gone with girlhood,
like an apparition, until one night
outside Woodstock, I heard shuffling in the branches
outside the kitchen window
and saw the glowing body, silver with time,
emerge from behind a lone pine.
I walked out the back door. Cold
air lifted my hair. We were so close
we almost touched. I was waiting for him to remember
who I was, to remember why he resented me.
Instead there was fear in his eyes. I could tell
he had been out there a long time.
He moved closer, his breath turning to steam.
I reached out and touched his cheek.
Like a child he heaved against me, and I held him.
In the silence there was a sick sister,
a crumpled house. I couldn't.
I thought about the long years between our last visit.
I wanted to explain how lonely I had been,
how loneliness had made me
mean, unreliable. Had driven me deeper in.
Even now, being with him
meant abandoning my family,
who were gathering inside the house,
waiting to serve dinner,
wondering where I was. I knew
he might never appear again,
or only after a long snow, in the middle of the night—
and that I would love him forever,
not in spite of the way he stayed gone
for so long, but because of it.

A lamp swings from a hook. Little rosettes
shine in the rain. I've done to men what she does to me,

but I don't tell her so. Instead, I run my fingers under
the metallic silver string which vanishes like a star

into her dark skirt. I stroke the soft hair,
pink in the light, silhouetted by tufts of frangipani

lining the bar. Once, I lived in a country
full of these flowers, where the old women boiled milk

and water on the street and spoke of desire
in a language I didn't understand. I lived

in a small room by the sea. Outside my window,
fruit dangled from a screw pine. It was beautiful

but I was afraid; I never opened the glass.

"I'm a Young Cowboy and Know I've Done Wrong" borrows its title from a line in the song "Streets of Laredo."

"From the Faraway, Nearby" takes its title from a Georgia O'Keefe painting.

"Alexei," "Tatiana," and "Mithridatism" are written in the imagined voice of Anastasia Romanov.

"Mithridatism" borrows the line "I get sick of just about everyone" from Kurt Vile's song "Baby's Arms."

"Deer in Bright Snow" responds to a line in the poem "You Cannot Rest" by Frank Bidart: "The trick was to give yourself only to what / could not receive what you had to give, // leaving you as you wished, free."

"Fawn Lake" was inspired by the poem "Sardines" by Henri Cole.

"The Gallery" paraphrases a line from Tom Healy's essay "Because a Fire Was in My Head" (2009): "Mark Rothko announced near the end of his life that it was his exuberantly colorful works, not the dark ones, that could be described as 'tragic.'"

"Winter Sister" is for Julia Anna Morrison.

"Dream Elegy" was written in memory of Will Morrison.

"University of Iowa Museum of Natural History" is for my godson, Félix Carlstein-Morrison.

"Blue Angels Air Show" borrows its title from a Bright Eyes song.

"March 9th, Dusk" was inspired by the poem "Signs" by Kai Carlson-Wee.

Thank you to the editors of the following publications, in which some of the poems in this book first appeared:

> *The Adroit Journal*: "Tatiana," "Winter Sister," "Floodplain"
> *The Antioch Review*: "In the Duty-Free Shop"
> *Bennington Review*: "August in the Adirondacks" and "Beacon" (now "At the Base of Mount Beacon")
> *The Best American Nonrequired Reading 2018*: "This Rain" (now "Fawn Lake")
> *Best New Poets 2020*: "Forest Horse"
> *Blunderbuss*: "Interlude: Summer House" (now: "Summer House")
> *B O D Y*: "Alexei," "Threnody"
> *Boston Review*: "I'm a Young Cowboy and Know I've Done Wrong"
> *The Common*: "Arrival"
> *The Cortland Review*: "Eidolon"
> *Great River Review*: "Dream Elegy" and "Frozen Water"
> *The Grief Diaries*: "Epilogue"
> *H.O.W. Journal*: "Grief"
> *The Iowa Review*: "Sub-Zero"
> *LAMBDA Literary*: "Riding the Bus Back to Oxford"
> *Leveler*: "Manhattan Ave"
> *Memorious*: "Mithridatism"
> *The Moth*: "Like Rain"
> *Narrative*: "At the Sunoco in West Virginia" and "Fly-Over States"
> *Pacifica Literary Review*: "University of Iowa Museum of Natural History"
> *Rattle*: "March 9th, Dusk"
> *Salmagundi*: "Master Bedroom," "In the Sulfur Baths"
> *Sixth Finch*: "This Rain" (now "Fawn Lake")
> *Tupelo Quarterly*: "From the Faraway, Nearby" and "Monhegan"

*

Thank you, Traci Brimhall, for choosing my manuscript (I am forever grateful). Thank you to Jon Tribble, the Crab Orchard Series editor, whose kindness I will always remember, and whose legacy lives on. To Jennifer Egan and the editors at Southern Illinois University Press, my deepest gratitude.

Thank you to Skidmore College, Columbia University's School of the Arts, and the University of Southern California. Thank you to the Fashion Institute of Technology for my first teaching job, and to the James Merrill House for my first residency.

To Peg Boyers, my beloved mentor, thank you. To Robert Boyers, and all my friends at the New York State Summer Writers Institute, my deepest love and thanks. This book would not exist without you.

Thank you to the teachers who shaped and encouraged my writing during the making of this book, especially April Bernard, Frank Bidart, Lucie Brock-Broido, Henri Cole, Timothy Donnelly, Kate Flint, Eamon Grennan, Dorothea Lasky, Phillip Lopate, Susan McCabe, Campbell McGrath, Honor Moore, Maggie Nelson, Danzy Senna, David St. John, and Mark Strand.

To all the friends who were an integral part of the years during which I wrote these poems, especially Kirsten Abel, Christopher Adamson, Ally Jane Ayers, Kim Bevan, Marina Blitshteyn, Natasha Blodgett, Synne Borgen, William Brewer, Allie Burns, Alex Dimitrov, Frances Dodds, Megan Fernandes, Amber Galeo, Kathy Geisel, Matthew Gellman, Hafizah Geter, Carlie Hoffman, Stephanie Horvath, Courtney Kampa, E. J. Koh, Muriel Leung, Michelle Lorenzutti, Elizabeth Metzger, Katharine Ogle, Anna Pipes, Hillary Reder, Austen Rosenfeld, Hana Sackler, Melissa Schlobohm, Ryann Stevenson, and writers Essy Stone, & Simone White —

*

Thank you Myra, Glen, Will, Laura, and John Morrison, for encouraging our imaginations.

Thank you to my godmother, Nancy Cook, for continued love and support.

Thank you to my parents, Clayton and Marjorie Pond, for radical encouragement and unconditional love.

Drew, I am always at home with you.

Dan Kraines, thank you for friendship, forever.

Kai Carlson-Wee, you are my happiness.

Julia Anna Morrison, my twin in everything, thank you. *For you I ring the bell sharp in my heart until you know it's me.*

Other Books in the Crab Orchard Series in Poetry